THE STARTING POINT LIBRARY

PEOPLE

Cousteau the Diver

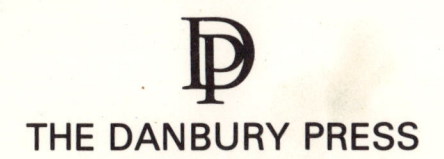

THE DANBURY PRESS

A Division of Grolier Enterprises, Inc.

©1973 Macdonald and Company (Publishers) Ltd.
First American Edition 1977
Library of Congress Catalog Card Number: 75-7418
Printed in U.S.A.

123456789987

sponge

These children are diving for sponges in Greece. They hold their breath under the water.

Klingert's
diving suit
1797

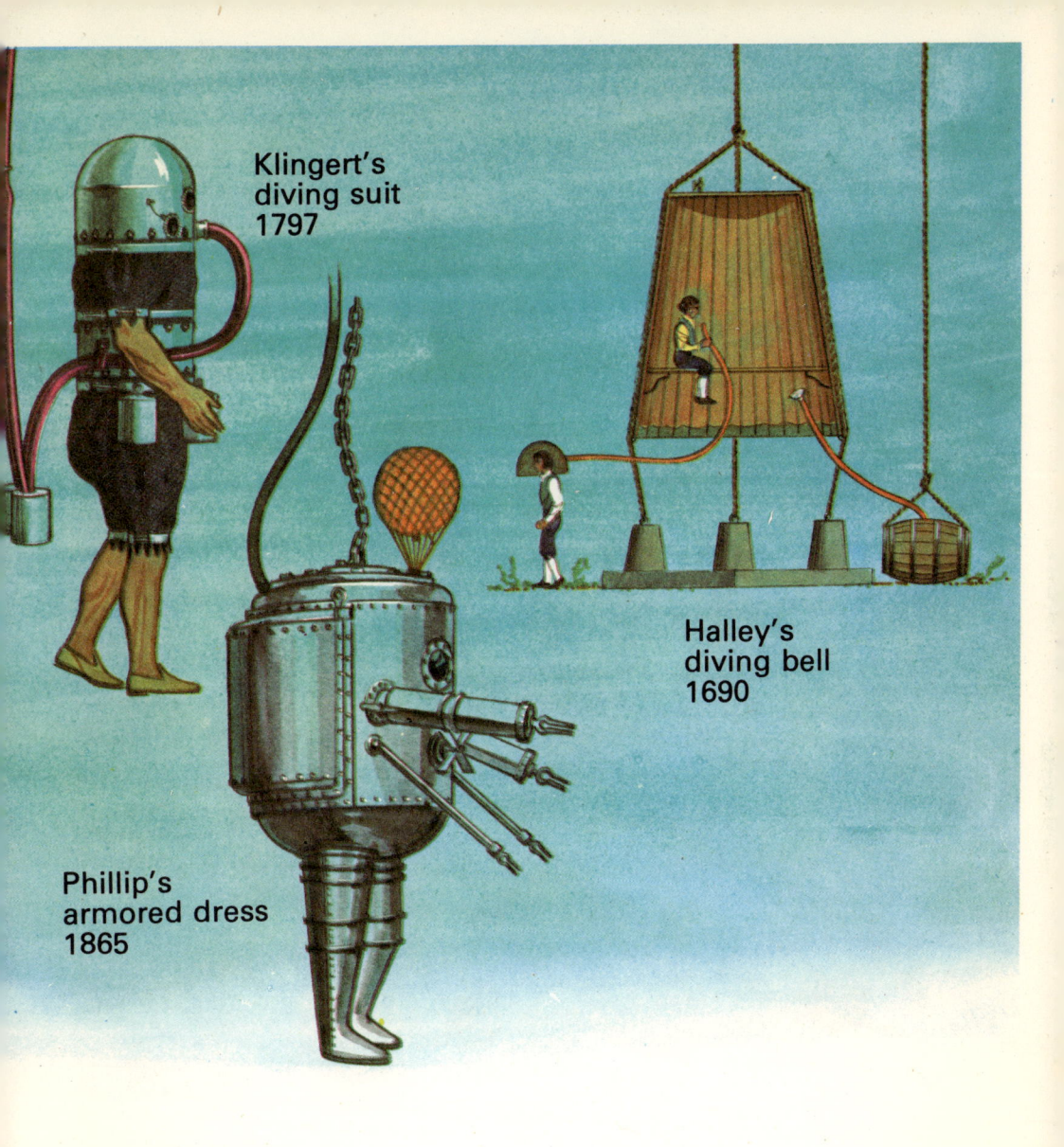

Halley's
diving bell
1690

Phillip's
armored dress
1865

People cannot breathe under water.
They need machines to give them air.
These are some early diving machines.
The divers could not move about easily.

grouper

Cousteau is a famous diver.
He was born in France.
When he was young
he joined the French navy.
He and his friends learned to dive.

parts of an aqualung

- breathing tube
- face mask
- air cylinder
- wet suit
- watch
- depth gauge
- snorkel tube
- weight belt
- fin

Cousteau invented the aqualung.
It lets divers breathe under water.
The diver carries air cylinders
on his back.
He breathes the air through tubes.

Cousteau and his friends explored the seabed.
They wore aqualungs.
They could swim under water like fishes.

They studied the plants
and animals that live in the sea.
They took many photographs.

Cousteau bought a ship
to go on diving expeditions.
It has a platform for divers.
The diving saucer is kept in the ship.
It is lowered into the water by crane.

The ship has an underwater room.
The divers can watch the sea animals.
Cousteau has travelled
all over the world in this ship.

9

airlift to move sand

wine jar

Cousteau has dived to look
for many sunken ships.
He found a Roman ship.
He brought up hundreds of wine jars.

Once he found a Spanish galleon.
It sank a long time ago.
Cousteau hoped to find treasure.
He found cannons and cannon balls.

humpback whale

man in balloon directs boat by radio

Cousteau wanted to find out how whales lived.
He followed them in his ship.

baby sperm whale

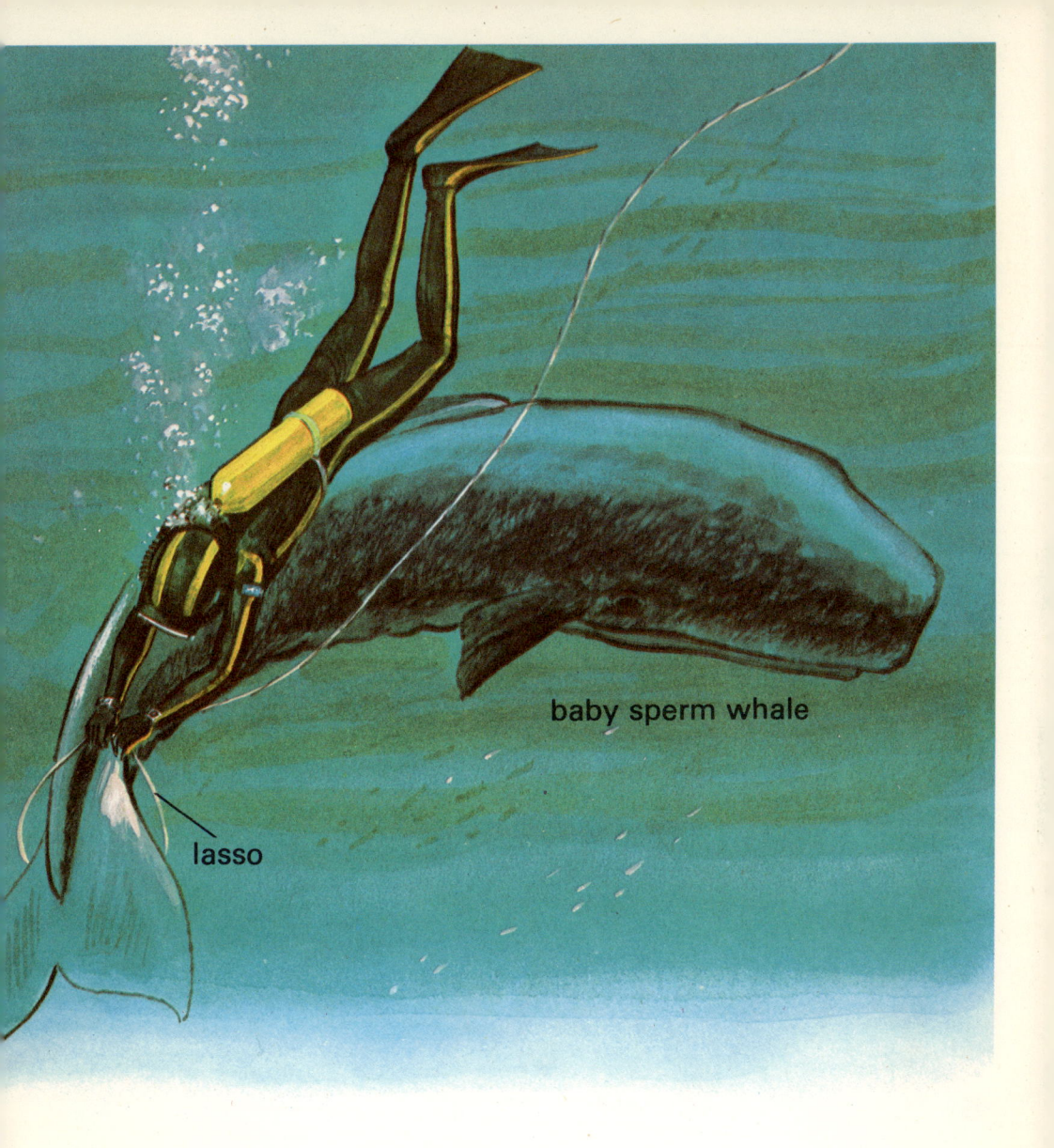

lasso

Some of his divers put metal markers
on the whales.
This helped the divers to track them.

Once Cousteau found a baby whale
stranded on a beach.
It was badly burned by the sun.
The divers lifted the whale on to the ship.

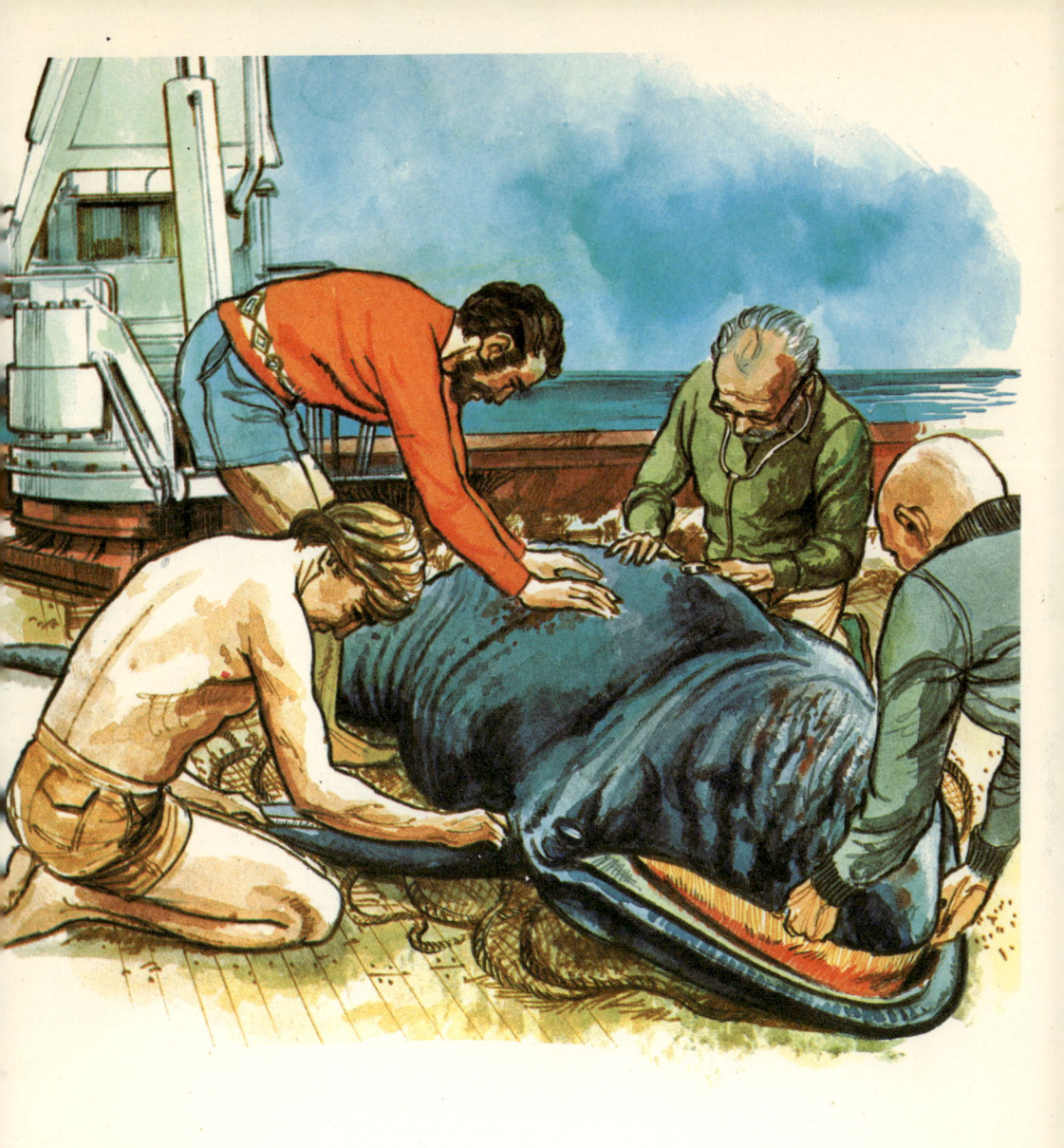

The divers fed it and bathed its burns.
They listened to its heartbeat.
They measured how long it was.

Cousteau has also watched dolphins.
Dolphins like to come near ships.
They leap high into the air.

anti-shark cage

Some of Cousteau's men feed sharks.
The sharks get very excited by food.
They can be very dangerous.
So the men stand in cages to feed
and photograph them.

pop-eyed
shark

This is a bathyscaphe.
It can go down deeper in the sea
than any other machine.
It has been to the bottom of the ocean.

Cousteau used this bathyscaphe
to explore deep parts of the sea.
He found pop-eyed sharks.

19

This is a 'floating island'.
Part of the tower is under water.
Scientists can watch fish swimming by without disturbing them.

diving saucer

portholes   inside the saucer

Cousteau invented this diving saucer.
Two divers can travel in it.
They can see through portholes.

21

Cousteau has explored coral reefs.
Some coral reefs are dying.
The divers wanted to find out why.

mirror

syringe

plastic
globe
for
storing
fish

The divers collected pieces of coral to study.
Some of the divers travelled on scooters.
They could move quickly underwater.

23

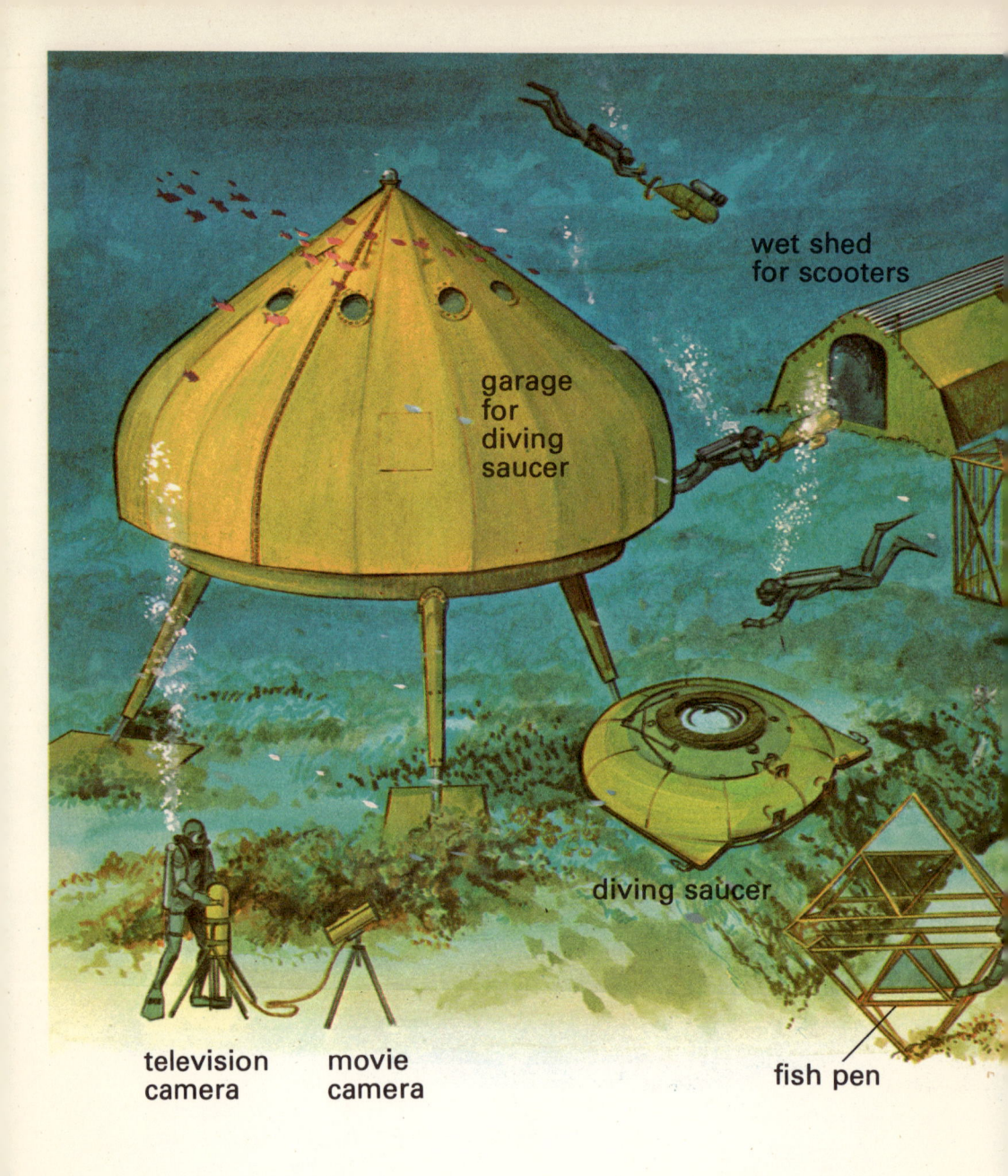

Cousteau and his men spent a month
living under the sea.
They lived in this Starfish House.

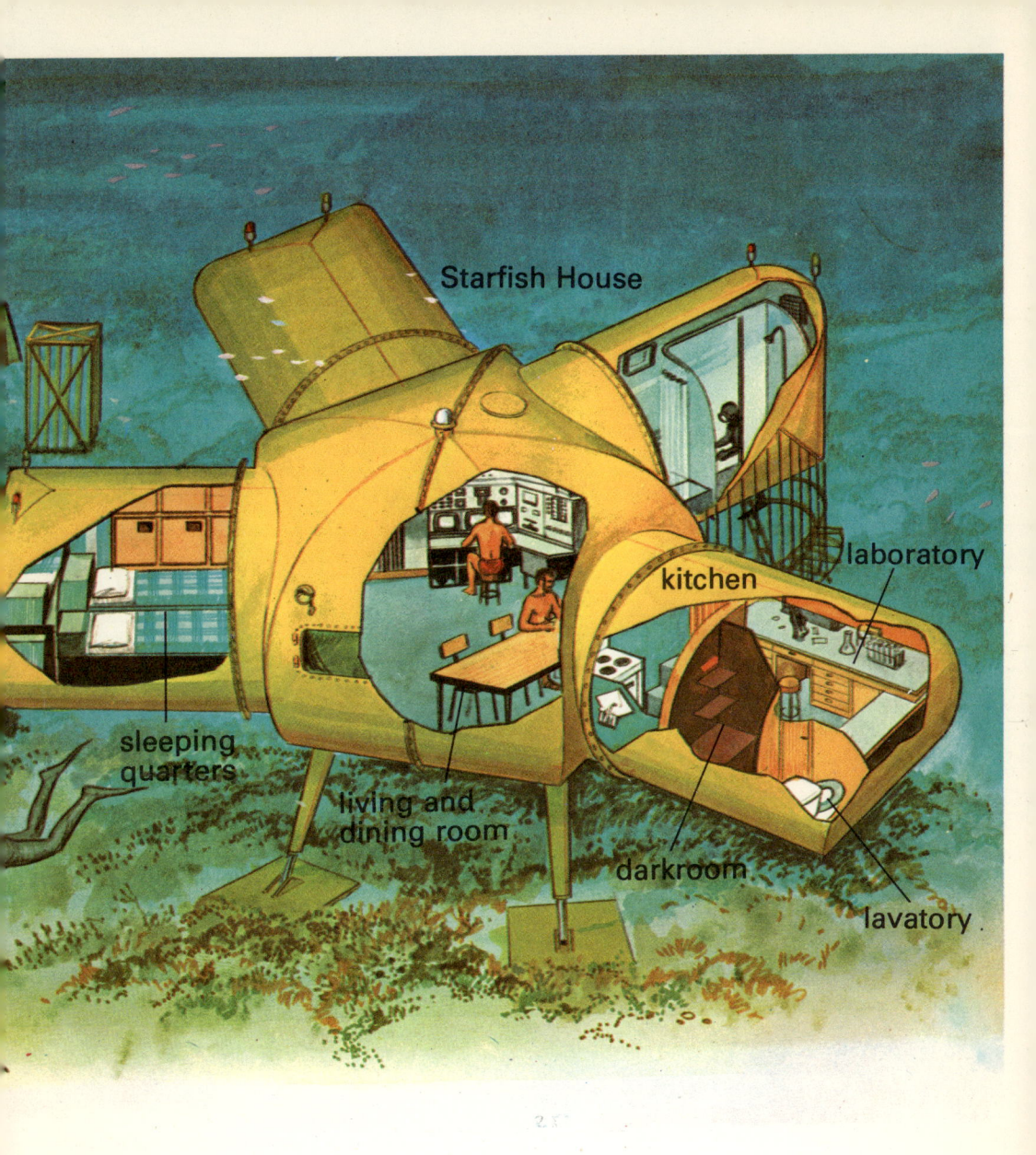

During the day they collected
fish and rocks.
Cousteau thinks that one day
people will live in towns under the sea.

glass

paper

tape

See for yourself how a diving bell works.
Stick some paper into the bottom of a glass.
Push the glass in the water, like this.
How far up does the water come?
Try this with different shaped glasses.

Index

sponge
(page 2)

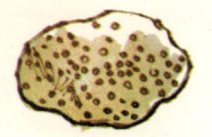

aqualung
(page 5)

cylinder
(page 5)

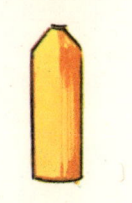

galleon
(page 11)

cannon
(page 11)

whale
(page 12)

dolphin
(page 16)

shark
(page 17)

bathyscaphe
(page 18)

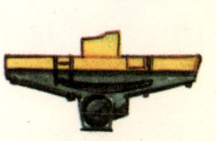

diving saucer
(page 21)

porthole
(page 21)

coral
(page 22)

Facts about divers

333 B.C.   Alexander the Great dived in a diving bell.

1535 A.D.   A diving bell was used to explore sunken Roman galleys.

1690   Halley invented a way to renew the air in diving bells.

1715   John Lethbridge made the first diving suit.

1797   Klingert designed the first airtight diving suit.

1819   Siebe made a diving suit with an air pump

1930   Beebe and Barton descended in the first bathysphere.

1943   Cousteau and Gagnon tried out the first aqualung.

1948   Piccard descended in the first bathyscaphe.

1963   Cousteau built and lived in an underwater village.